Rebecca Wingard-Nelson

Enslow Publishers, Inc.

40 Industrial Road	PO Box 38
Box 398	Aldershot
Berkeley Heights, NJ 07922	Hants GU12 6BP
USA	UK

http://www.enslow.com

Library of Congress Cataloging-in-Publication Data

Wingard-Nelson, Rebecca.
Trigonometry / Rebecca Wingard-Nelson.
     v. cm. — (Math success)
     Includes bibliographical references and index.
     Contents: Lines and angles — Angles and their measure — Triangles — Congruent
triangles — Identifying congruent triangles — Ratios and proportions — Similar triangles
— Right triangles — Square roots — The pythagorean theorem — Using the pythagorean
theorem — The converse of the pythagorean theorem — Trigonometric ratios —
Trigonometry of right triangles — All from one — Complements and cofunctions —
Reciprocal identities — Trigonometry tables and calculators — Sine, cosecant and side
length — Cosine, secant, and side length — Tangent, cotangent and side length — Finding
the angle measure — The trigonometric pythagorean theorem — Isosceles right triangles —
30-60-90 triangles — The unit circle — Radians and degrees — Signs of trigonometric
functions.
     ISBN 0-7660-2568-3 (hardcover)
     1. Geometry—Juvenile literature. 2. Trigonometry—Juvenile literature.
[1. Geometry. 2. Trigonometry.] I. Title. II. Series.
     QA445.5.w555   2004
     516—dc22

                          2003027619

Printed in the United States of America

10 9 8 7 6 5 4 3 2

To Our Readers: We have done our best to make sure all Internet Addresses in this book were
active and appropriate when we went to press. However, the author and the publisher have no
control over and assume no liability for the material available on those Internet sites or on other
Web sites they may link to. Any comments or suggestions can be sent by e-mail to
comments@enslow.com or to the address on the back cover.

Cover illustration (background): © Corel Corporation

Contents

Introduction

If you were to look up the meaning of the word *mathematics,* you would find that it is the study of numbers, quantities, and shapes and how they relate to each other.

Mathematics is important to all world cultures, including our world of work. The following are just some of the ways in which studying math will help you:

- ▶ You will know how much money you are spending.
- ▶ You will know if the cashier has given you the right amount of change.
- ▶ You will know how to use measurements to build things.
- ▶ Your science classes will be easier and more interesting.
- ▶ You will understand music on a whole new level.
- ▶ You will be able to qualify for and land a rewarding job.

Trigonometry is a branch of mathematics that studies the measurements of triangles and how their sides and angles relate to each other. Distances that are difficult to measure, such as the distance from the earth to the moon or across a lake, can be found using trigonometry. Sound vibrations and the flow of electrical currents also use applications of trigonometric functions.

This book has been written so that you can learn about trigonometry at your own speed. You can use this book on your own, or work with a friend, tutor, or parent.

Good luck and have fun!

1. Lines and Angles

Trigonometry and geometry use words that describe different kinds of lines and angles that are used to make figures.

Lines

A line extends in two directions and does not end. A line is always straight. Arrows are used to show that a figure is a line. Lines are named using two points on the line.

This line is written $\overleftrightarrow{AB}$, and is read "line AB."

A line segment is part of a line and has two endpoints. This line segment is written $\overline{CD}$ and is read "line segment CD."

A ray is also part of a line. It has one endpoint but does not end in the other direction. This ray is written $\overrightarrow{EF}$ and is read "ray EF."

Lines, line segments, and rays may cross, or intersect. When they intersect and form a right angle, or square corner, they are called perpendicular. If they do not intersect no matter how far they are extended, they are called parallel.

Line segments that do not cross are not always parallel. They are only parallel if they will never cross, no matter how far they are extended.

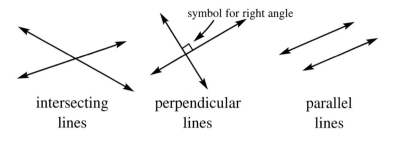

| intersecting lines | perpendicular lines | parallel lines |

Angles

When two lines intersect, angles are formed. These angles will share the same endpoint. The shared endpoint is called the vertex.

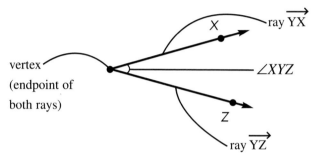

Two rays (or line segments) are the sides of each angle. To name an angle, use a point on each ray or line segment and the vertex. The vertex letter must be the middle letter in the name. This angle can be named ∠XYZ, which is read "angle XYZ," or ∠ZYX, which is read "angle ZYX."

When it will not be confusing, angles may be named using only the vertex. This angle could be called ∠Y, which is read "angle Y."

When two lines cross, four angles are formed. All four angles have the same vertex.

2. Angles and Their Measure

Angles can be described by their size. They are measured in units called degrees. The symbol for degrees is °.

Measuring Angles

Angles are measured using a protractor. When you use a protractor, place it so that the hole in the center of the straight edge is over the vertex. Align one side of the angle with the line on the protractor that crosses the hole. Read the number where the other side of the angle passes under the protractor.

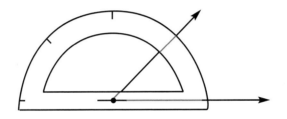

Right angles are angles like the corner of a square or rectangle. They are labeled with a small corner shape.

Right angles have a measure of exactly 90°.

90°

If you do not have a protractor, use an index card to help you decide if an angle is acute, right, obtuse, or straight.

Acute angles are angles that are smaller than right angles.

Straight angles are straight lines.

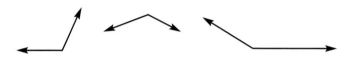

Obtuse angles are larger than right angles, but smaller than straight angles.

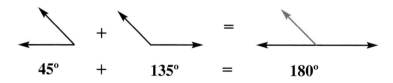

Adding Angles

Angles can be added together to form new angles. Two angles that add up to 90° are called complementary angles.

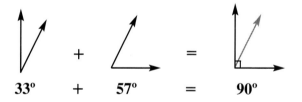

| 33° | + | 57° | = | 90° |

Two angles that add up to 180° are called supplementary angles.

| 45° | + | 135° | = | 180° |

All complementary angles are acute.
A complete circle has 360°.

3. Triangles

A triangle has three sides and three angles. You can name a triangle using the symbol for a triangle, △, and then listing the vertices of the triangle in any order you choose. This triangle can be named △ABC.

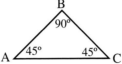

The sum of the angles in a triangle is always 180°. When you know two of the angle measures in a triangle, you can find the third angle measure.

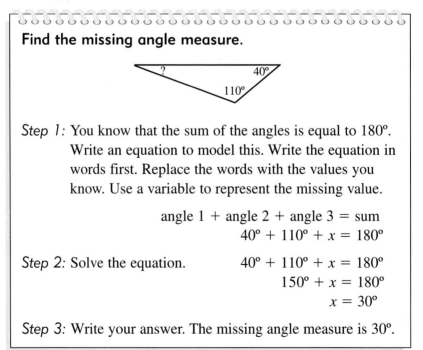

Find the missing angle measure.

Step 1: You know that the sum of the angles is equal to 180°. Write an equation to model this. Write the equation in words first. Replace the words with the values you know. Use a variable to represent the missing value.

$$\text{angle } 1 + \text{angle } 2 + \text{angle } 3 = \text{sum}$$
$$40° + 110° + x = 180°$$

Step 2: Solve the equation.
$$40° + 110° + x = 180°$$
$$150° + x = 180°$$
$$x = 30°$$

Step 3: Write your answer. The missing angle measure is 30°.

The sum of the angles of any triangle is 180°.

Classifying Triangles

Tringles can be classified by the measure of their angles.

An acute triangle has three acute angles (each is less than 90°).

A right triangle has exactly one right angle.

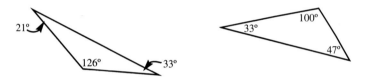

An obtuse triangle has exactly one obtuse angle (one angle greater than 90°).

Triangles can also be classified by their sides.

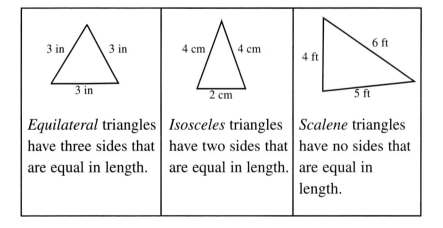

Equilateral triangles have three sides that are equal in length.	*Isosceles* triangles have two sides that are equal in length.	*Scalene* triangles have no sides that are equal in length.

A triangle can have only one right angle. A triangle can have only one obtuse angle. A triangle may have two or three acute angles.

4. Congruent Triangles

Triangles are congruent when they have the same shape and size.

Look at these two triangles. If you placed one on top of the other, you would see they are exactly the same size and shape.

$\triangle ABC$ and $\triangle DEF$ are congruent. The symbol for congruence is $\cong$. You can say $\triangle ABC \cong \triangle DEF$. The vertices of the two triangles are listed in corresponding, or matching order.

Congruent Parts

Congruent triangles have corresponding, or matching, angles that are congruent. If the triangles shown were placed on top of each other and aligned, $\angle A$ and $\angle D$ would be in the same position. This makes $\angle A$ and $\angle D$ congruent corresponding angles. Angles that are congruent have the same measure.

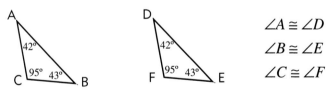

$$\angle A \cong \angle D$$
$$\angle B \cong \angle E$$
$$\angle C \cong \angle F$$

Angle congruence is shown using small curved lines for the matching angles.

congruent figures—Figures that have the same size and shape.
Corresponding means "matching."

Corresponding sides of congruent triangles have the same measure.

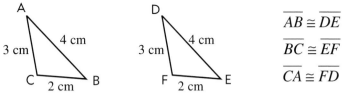

$$\overline{AB} \cong \overline{DE}$$
$$\overline{BC} \cong \overline{EF}$$
$$\overline{CA} \cong \overline{FD}$$

Small straight lines are used to show congruence on the matching sets of sides. Sides $\overline{AC}$ and $\overline{DF}$ are corresponding sides.

Triangles ΔKLM and ΔRST are congruent. Find the value of x.

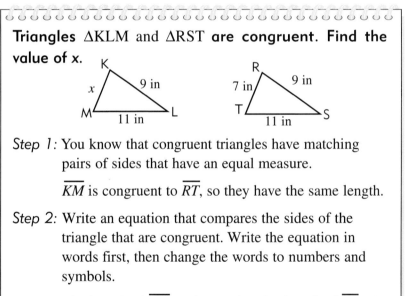

Step 1: You know that congruent triangles have matching pairs of sides that have an equal measure.

$\overline{KM}$ is congruent to $\overline{RT}$, so they have the same length.

Step 2: Write an equation that compares the sides of the triangle that are congruent. Write the equation in words first, then change the words to numbers and symbols.

The length of $\overline{KM}$ (x) is equal to the length of $\overline{RT}$ (7).
$$x = 7$$

Step 3: Solve for x. This equation $x = 7$
is already solved for x.

Triangles can be turned in different directions and still be congruent.

5. Identifying Congruent Triangles

You can tell when triangles are congruent without knowing all of their measurements. There are four rules you can use to compare corresponding parts of two triangles to show they are congruent.

Side-Side-Side (SSS) Rule

When all of the corresponding sides in a triangle have the same measurement, the two triangles are congruent. This rule is abbreviated SSS.

Side-Angle-Side (SAS) Rule

When triangles have two pairs of congruent sides and a pair of congruent angles between them, the triangles are congruent.

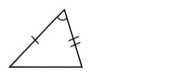

Angle-Side-Angle (ASA) Rule

When triangles have two pairs of congruent angles and a pair of congruent sides between them, the triangles are congruent.

The triangle congruency rules can start on any part of the triangle and move clockwise or counterclockwise. It might look like AAS instead of SAA, but the rule still works.

Side-Angle-Angle (SAA) Rule

When two triangles have two pairs of congruent angles and one pair of corresponding congruent sides that are not between the two angles, the triangles are congruent.

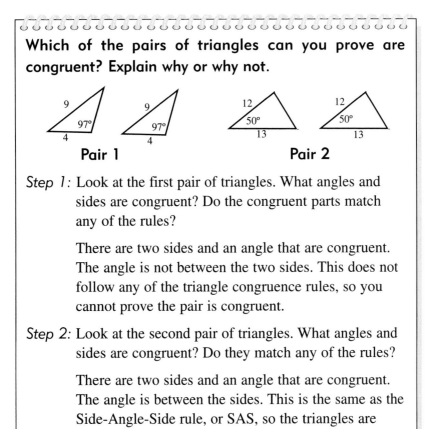

Which of the pairs of triangles can you prove are congruent? Explain why or why not.

Pair 1

Pair 2

Step 1: Look at the first pair of triangles. What angles and sides are congruent? Do the congruent parts match any of the rules?

There are two sides and an angle that are congruent. The angle is not between the two sides. This does not follow any of the triangle congruence rules, so you cannot prove the pair is congruent.

Step 2: Look at the second pair of triangles. What angles and sides are congruent? Do they match any of the rules?

There are two sides and an angle that are congruent. The angle is between the sides. This is the same as the Side-Angle-Side rule, or SAS, so the triangles are congruent.

I can follow these rules!

6. Ratios and Proportions

Ratios

A ratio is a comparison of two quantities. The length of one side of a figure can be compared to the length of another side of a figure using a ratio.

3 cm

10 cm

The ratio of length to width for the rectangle is 10 to 3.

Ratios can be written in three ways, but they are always read in the same way. This ratio is read "10 to 3".

$$10 \text{ to } 3 \qquad 10:3 \qquad \frac{10}{3}$$

When ratios are written as fractions, they can be reduced to lowest terms.

Write the ratio for the length of side *a* to the length of side *b* in lowest terms.

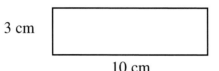

$b = 15$ $a = 5$

$c = 18$

Step 1: Write the ratio of side *a* to side *b* as a fraction. $\dfrac{5}{15}$

Step 2: Change the fraction to lowest terms. $\dfrac{5}{15} = \dfrac{1}{3}$

Ratios do not need to have the same units. You can set up a ratio for the number of chairs to the number of people, or the number of books to the number of classrooms.

Equal ratios are ratios that reduce to the same fraction in lowest terms.

$$\frac{12}{4} \text{ reduces to } \frac{3}{1}, \text{ and } \frac{9}{3} \text{ reduces to } \frac{3}{1}$$

$\frac{12}{4}$ and $\frac{9}{3}$ are equal ratios.

Proportions

A proportion is an equation that says that two ratios are equal.

$$\frac{1}{2} = \frac{3}{6}$$

When two ratios are equal, their corresponding parts are proportional. The ratio of numerator to numerator is proportional to the ratio of denominator to denominator.

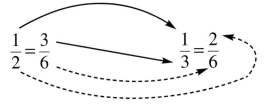

You can tell quickly if two ratios are proportional by taking their cross products. The cross products are found by multiplying in a crisscross pattern. If the cross products are equal, then the two ratios are proportional.

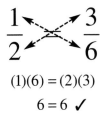

$$(1)(6) = (2)(3)$$
$$6 = 6 \checkmark$$

The cross products are equal, so the ratios are proportional.

When two ratios can be reduced to the same lowest terms, they are called proportional.

Two triangles are similar if they have the same shape. They do not need to be the same size.

In similar triangles, the corresponding angles are congruent. Below, $\angle A \cong \angle X$. The symbol for similarity is $\sim$.

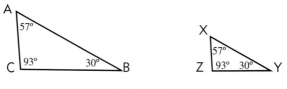

$$\triangle ABC \sim \triangle XYZ$$

Similar triangles do not need to have congruent sides. However, all three pairs of corresponding sides in similar triangles will have the same ratio.

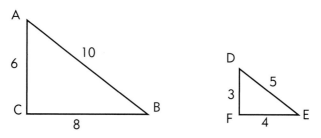

Side $\overline{AB}$ corresponds to side $\overline{DE}$. The length of side $\overline{AB}$ is 10 units. The length of side $\overline{DE}$ is 5 units.

The ratio of side $\overline{AB}$ to side $\overline{DE}$ is 10:5, or 2:1.

Side $\overline{BC}$ corresponds to side $\overline{EF}$. The ratio is 8:4, or 2:1.

Side $\overline{CA}$ corresponds to side $\overline{FD}$. The ratio is 6:3, or 2:1.

The ratios for the pairs of sides are equal.

$\overline{AB}:\overline{DE} = \overline{BC}:\overline{EF} = \overline{CA}:\overline{FD} = 2:1$.

A ratio compares one number to another. Ratios can be written in three ways, 1 to 10, 1:10, or $\frac{1}{10}$.

ΔLMN ~ ΔRST. **Find the length of $\overline{ST}$.**

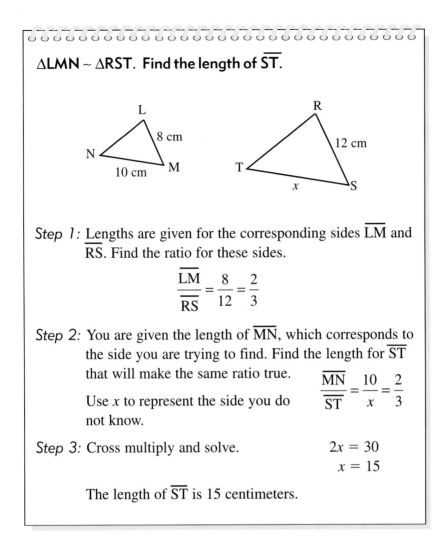

Step 1: Lengths are given for the corresponding sides $\overline{LM}$ and $\overline{RS}$. Find the ratio for these sides.

$$\frac{\overline{LM}}{\overline{RS}} = \frac{8}{12} = \frac{2}{3}$$

Step 2: You are given the length of $\overline{MN}$, which corresponds to the side you are trying to find. Find the length for $\overline{ST}$ that will make the same ratio true.

Use x to represent the side you do not know.

$$\frac{\overline{MN}}{\overline{ST}} = \frac{10}{x} = \frac{2}{3}$$

Step 3: Cross multiply and solve.

$$2x = 30$$
$$x = 15$$

The length of $\overline{ST}$ is 15 centimeters.

Remember: Triangles that are congruent or similar are named with their matching vertices in order.

8. Right Triangles

Right triangles are special triangles. A right triangle has one angle that is exactly 90° and two angles that are each less than 90°. The right angle is normally labeled with a small corner shape. When you see the corner on a triangle, you know it is a right triangle.

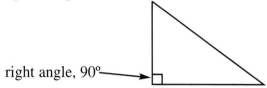

right angle, 90°———→

The two line segments that form the right angle are called legs. The side of the triangle that is across from the right angle is called the hypotenuse. The hypotenuse is always the longest side.

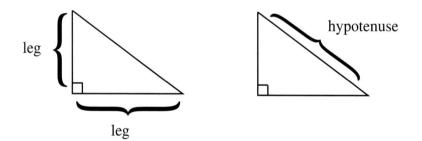

leg {

leg

hypotenuse

The two acute angles in a right triangle always add up to 90°. You already know that the three angles of a triangle add up to 180° and that the right angle in a right triangle is 90°. Therefore, the sum of the two other angles must be 90°.

acute angle—An angle that measures less than 90°.
hypotenuse—The side of a right triangle that is opposite the right angle.

When you know one of the acute angles in a right triangle, you can always find the other one.

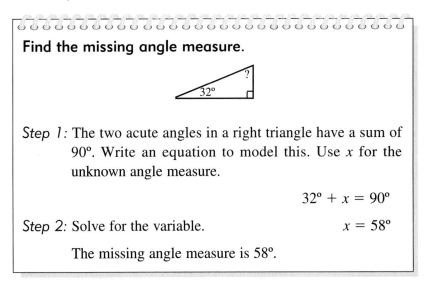

Find the missing angle measure.

Step 1: The two acute angles in a right triangle have a sum of 90°. Write an equation to model this. Use x for the unknown angle measure.

$$32° + x = 90°$$

Step 2: Solve for the variable. $x = 58°$

The missing angle measure is 58°.

Similarity in Right Triangles

In right triangles, you only need to know that one pair of acute angles is congruent to know that the triangles are similar. Let's see why this is true.

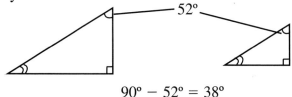

$$90° - 52° = 38°$$

In right triangles, the two acute angles add up to 90°. The triangle on the left has one acute angle that is 52°. The other angle must be 90° − 52°, or 38°. The triangle on the right also has one acute angle that is 52°, so the other must be 38°.

Each triangle has angles that measure 38°, 52°, and 90°. Triangles with three corresponding congruent angles are similar.

See pages 18 and 19 for more on similar triangles.

9. Square Roots

In solving many trigonometry problems, squares and square roots are used. The square of a number is the number multiplied by itself. The first number below is read "3 squared."

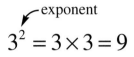

$$3^2 = 3 \times 3 = 9$$

If you think of a geometrical square, you can see that

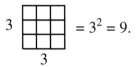

$$3 \quad = 3^2 = 9.$$

Square Roots

The symbol for "square root" is the radical sign. The square root is the number that when multiplied by itself gives the number that is under the radical sign.

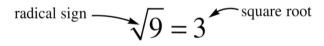

radical sign $\longrightarrow \sqrt{9} = 3 \longleftarrow$ square root

The square root of 9 is 3.

Perfect Squares

A perfect square is a number such as 1, 4, 9, 16, or 25 that has a whole number as its square root.

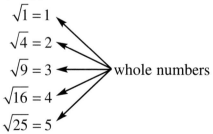

$$\sqrt{1} = 1$$
$$\sqrt{4} = 2$$
$$\sqrt{9} = 3 \longleftarrow \text{whole numbers}$$
$$\sqrt{16} = 4$$
$$\sqrt{25} = 5$$

exponent—A number that tells you how many times to multiply a given number by itself.
square—A number with an exponent of 2.

Radicals

Numbers that include the radical sign are sometimes called radicals.

radical ⟶ $\sqrt{32}$

When a radical does not contain a perfect square, you still may be able to simplify the radical. First see if any of its factors is a perfect square, then solve. Leave the remaining factor as a radical.

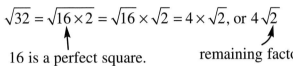

$$\sqrt{32} = \sqrt{16 \times 2} = \sqrt{16} \times \sqrt{2} = 4 \times \sqrt{2}, \text{ or } 4\sqrt{2}$$

16 is a perfect square.   remaining factor

Simplify the radical $\sqrt{120}$.

Step 1: Find any perfect squares that are factors of 120.

4 is a factor of 120, and 4 is a perfect square.
$$4 \times 30 = 120$$

30 is still a pretty large number, so find the factors of 30.

$$30 = 2 \times 3 \times 5$$

Since there are no factors that happen more than once, there are no more perfect squares.

Step 2: Solve for the perfect square. Write the square root outside the radical sign, and leave the remaining factor under the radical sign.

$$\sqrt{120} = \sqrt{4 \times 30} = \sqrt{4} \times \sqrt{30} = 2\sqrt{30}$$
$$\sqrt{120} = 2\sqrt{30}$$

factor—A number that is multiplied to find a product. For example:

2 and 4 are factors of 8 because 2 x 4 = 8.

10. The Pythagorean Theorem

The Pythagorean theorem is a formula about right triangles. It was discovered in Greece by a man named Pythagoras in the sixth century B.C.

In the figure below, the letter c is used to represent the hypotenuse. The remaining two legs are represented by a and b. It does not matter which leg is labeled a and which is labeled b.

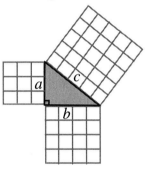

Pythagoras said that if you draw a square on the length of side a and another on side b, the sum of their areas will equal the area of a square drawn on the hypotenuse. His theorem is written as the equation $a^2 + b^2 = c^2$.

In other words, when you know the length of two sides of a right triangle, you can find the length of the third side using the Pythagorean theorem.

A right triangle has one leg that is 3 inches long and another leg that is 4 inches long. What is the length of the hypotenuse?

Be careful to always use the length of the hypotenuse for the c value. It will help you if you remember that the hypotenuse is the longest of the three sides.

Step 1: Since the triangle is a right triangle, you can use the Pythagorean theorem to find the missing side length. Replace a and b with values that you are given, 3 and 4.

$$a^2 + b^2 = c^2$$
$$3^2 + 4^2 = c^2$$

Step 2: Solve for c.

Apply the exponents. $\qquad\qquad 9 + 16 = c^2$

Add. $\qquad\qquad\qquad\qquad\quad 25 = c^2$

Take the square root of both sides. $\qquad \sqrt{25} = \sqrt{c^2}$

The hypotenuse is 5 inches long. $\qquad\quad 5 = c$

A right triangle has one leg that is 21 inches long. The hypotenuse is 29 inches long. What is the length of the other leg?

Step 1: Use the Pythagorean theorem to find the missing side length. Replace the variables with values you know. Let the leg you know be side a, $a = 21$. The hypotenuse is always c, so c = 29.

$$a^2 + b^2 = c^2$$
$$21^2 + b^2 = 29^2$$

Step 2: Solve for b.

Apply the exponents. $\qquad\qquad\qquad 441 + b^2 = 841$

Subtract to get b alone. $\quad 441 - 441 + b^2 = 841 - 441$

Take the square root of both sides. $\qquad\qquad b^2 = 400$

$$b = \sqrt{400} = 20$$

The length of the other leg is 20 inches.

Some square roots are easy to find, but others are not. Use a calculator to find the square root of numbers that are difficult.

11. Using The Pythagorean Theorem

You can use the Pythagorean theorem many ways in the real world. You can decide if a couch will fit through a hallway with a right turn in it, or what the dimensions of a staircase need to be.

A shed has a roof that is 12 feet above the ground at the lowest edge. The base of the ladder must be at least 4 feet away from the shed to be safe. Will a 14-foot ladder be tall enough to reach the roof?

Step 1: Draw a sketch that models the problem.

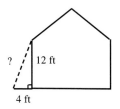

?   12 ft

4 ft

Step 2: You need to decide if the hypotenuse of the right triangle that is formed by the ground and the shed is 14 feet or less. Use the Pythagorean theorem and substitute the lengths of the sides you know for *a* and *b*. Let $a = 4$ and $b = 12$.

$$a^2 + b^2 = c^2$$
$$4^2 + 12^2 = c^2$$

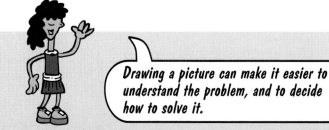

Drawing a picture can make it easier to understand the problem, and to decide how to solve it.

Step 3: Solve for c.

$$16 + 144 = c^2$$
$$160 = c^2$$
$$\sqrt{160} = c$$
$$12.649 \approx c$$

Step 4: Answer the question in the problem. The ladder is 14 feet long. Is that long enough to reach the roof safely?

Yes, a 14-foot ladder is longer than 12.649 feet, so it is long enough to reach the roof safely.

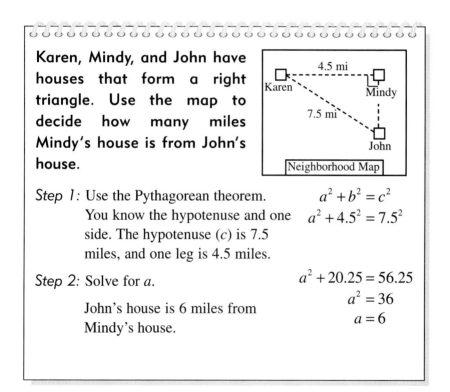

Karen, Mindy, and John have houses that form a right triangle. Use the map to decide how many miles Mindy's house is from John's house.

Step 1: Use the Pythagorean theorem. You know the hypotenuse and one side. The hypotenuse (c) is 7.5 miles, and one leg is 4.5 miles.

$$a^2 + b^2 = c^2$$
$$a^2 + 4.5^2 = 7.5^2$$

Step 2: Solve for a.

$$a^2 + 20.25 = 56.25$$
$$a^2 = 36$$
$$a = 6$$

John's house is 6 miles from Mindy's house.

The symbol $\approx$ means "approximately equal to." It is used whenever a number is rounded, or estimated.

12. The Converse of the Pythagorean Theorem

The Pythagorean theorem says

> **if** a triangle is a right triangle,
> **then** the sides will always make the equation
> $a^2 + b^2 = c^2$ true.

The converse of a statement reverses the order. The converse of the Pythagorean theorem is still true. It says

> **if** a triangle has sides that make the equation
> $a^2 + b^2 = c^2$ true,
> **then** the triangle is a right triangle.

If you can show that $a^2 + b^2 = c^2$ is true in a triangle, then you will know the triangle is a right triangle.

Show that a triangle whose sides are 5 cm, 12 cm, and 13 cm is a right triangle.

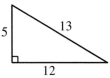

Step 1: The longest side is the hypotenuse. The hypotenuse is the side that is 13 units long.

Step 2: Substitute the lengths into the Pythagorean theorem.
$$a^2 + b^2 = c^2$$
$$5^2 + 12^2 = 13^2$$

Remember: The hypotenuse is the side that is directly across from the right angle. It is also the longest side.

Step 3: Solve.

$$5^2 + 12^2 = 13^2$$
$$25 + 144 = 169$$
$$169 = 169$$

Step 4: Compare the numbers on both sides of the equal sign. Is the statement true? $169 = 169$

Yes, the equation is true, so the triangle is a right triangle.

Using the Converse

Carpenters and other construction workers use the converse of the Pythagorean theorem every day. Many times a floor, a cabinet, or a door or window frame needs to be checked for right angles.

A 3-4-5 triangle is used, or a triangle with sides that are 3 units, 4 units, and 5 units long. The units are small and easy to work with; and $3^2 + 4^2 = 5^2$, so it forms a right triangle.

On one side of a corner, 3 units, usually inches, are measured and marked. On the other side of the corner, 4 units are measured and marked. A final measurement is taken from the mark on one side to the mark on the other. If the measurement is 5 units, the corner is a 90-degree angle.

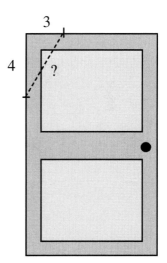

Measure 3 inches and 4 inches along the sides of a corner of a piece of paper. Mark the measurements, and then measure from one mark to the other. Is the corner of your paper a right angle?

13. Trigonometric Ratios

The sides and acute angles in a right triangle can be compared using six ratios.

The longest side of a right triangle has already been named as the hypotenuse. The other two sides are named in reference to one of the acute angles. Because geometry and trigonometry were developed by the ancient Greeks, Greek letters are usually used to name the acute angles. The Greek letter theta, θ, is a typical variable that you will see used for angle measure.

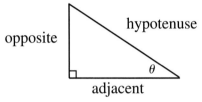

The adjacent leg and the hypotenuse are the sides of angle θ. The leg that is directly across from angle θ is called the opposite leg. These three terms—opposite, adjacent, and hypotenuse—are used to state the trigonometric functions.

Trigonometric Functions

$$\text{sine of } \theta = \sin \theta = \frac{\text{opposite}}{\text{hypotenuse}} \qquad \text{cosecant of } \theta = \csc \theta = \frac{\text{hypotenuse}}{\text{opposite}}$$

$$\text{cosine of } \theta = \cos \theta = \frac{\text{adjacent}}{\text{hypotenuse}} \qquad \text{secant of } \theta = \sec \theta = \frac{\text{hypotenuse}}{\text{adjacent}}$$

$$\text{tangent of } \theta = \tan \theta = \frac{\text{opposite}}{\text{adjacent}} \qquad \text{cotangent of } \theta = \cot \theta = \frac{\text{adjacent}}{\text{opposite}}$$

The functions on the right side are the reciprocal of the functions on the left.

Remember: Right triangles have two acute angles. Be very careful you are naming the adjacent and opposite sides in relation to the specified angle.

The sine, cosine, and tangent functions are the most commonly used functions.

It is helpful to make up a sentence or phrase to remind you which trigonometric name goes with each ratio. One sentence you can use is

Sister Olive Had Coats And Hats To Offer All.

$$\text{Sine } \theta = \frac{\text{Opposite}}{\text{Hypotenuse}} \quad \text{Cosine } \theta = \frac{\text{Adjacent}}{\text{Hypotenuse}} \quad \text{Tangent } \theta = \frac{\text{Opposite}}{\text{Adjacent}}$$

The sides of a right triangle are given in the diagram. Name and find the value of the six trigonometric functions for the angle θ.

17   θ 8

15

Step 1: Look at the diagram and decide what sides are adjacent, opposite, and the hypotenuse.

The longest side, 17, is the hypotenuse.
The leg that is part of the angle, 8, is the adjacent side.
The leg that is opposite θ, 15, is the opposite side.

Step 2: Name each of the trigonometric functions and substitute in the lengths of the sides.

$$\sin \theta = \frac{\text{opposite}}{\text{hypotenuse}} = \frac{15}{17} \qquad \csc \theta = \frac{\text{hypotenuse}}{\text{opposite}} = \frac{17}{15}$$

$$\cos \theta = \frac{\text{adjacent}}{\text{hypotenuse}} = \frac{8}{17} \qquad \sec \theta = \frac{\text{hypotenuse}}{\text{adjacent}} = \frac{17}{8}$$

$$\tan \theta = \frac{\text{opposite}}{\text{adjacent}} = \frac{15}{8} \qquad \cot \theta = \frac{\text{adjacent}}{\text{opposite}} = \frac{8}{15}$$

Once you have the sides named, you can just substitute in the numbers!

14. Trigonometry of Right Triangles

A right triangle can be formed by drawing a line that is perpendicular to the initial side of an acute angle. The initial side of the angle is the side from which you begin measuring the acute angle. The terminal side of the angle is where the measurement ends.

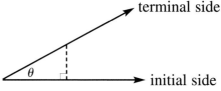

Any two right triangles that are formed using the acute angle will be similar. They will have corresponding sides with ratios that are equal. From the triangles below, the following ratios are true.

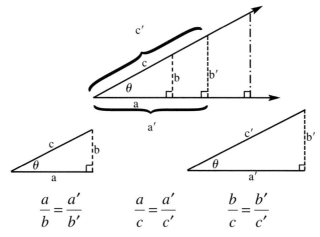

$$\frac{a}{b} = \frac{a'}{b'} \qquad \frac{a}{c} = \frac{a'}{c'} \qquad \frac{b}{c} = \frac{b'}{c'}$$

Side c and side c' are both hypotenuse sides. Sides b and b' are both opposite sides in reference to angle θ. Sides a and a' are both adjacent sides in reference to angle θ.

More about similarity and right triangles is covered in Chapter 7.

Let's see what happens when we look at the sine ratio in two similar triangles.

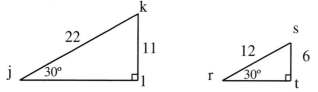

The sine function is $\sin \theta = \dfrac{\text{opposite}}{\text{hypotenuse}}$.

For $\triangle$ jkl, $\sin 30° = \dfrac{11}{22} = 0.5$ For $\triangle$ rst, $\sin 30° = \dfrac{6}{12} = 0.5$

The length of the sides of the triangle does not affect the trigonometric ratios. For every 30-degree angle, $\sin 30° = 0.5$. For every equal angle, the trigonometric ratios are equal.

Find the cosine of a 60-degree angle using the given triangle.

Step 1: The cosine function uses the adjacent leg and the hypotenuse. Write the function.

$\cos \theta = \dfrac{\text{adjacent}}{\text{hypotenuse}}$

Step 2: Replace the words with the values from the triangle.

$\cos 60° = \dfrac{6}{12} = 0.5$

The cosine of a 60-degree angle is 0.5.

The names of the right-triangle sides are often abbreviated.

opp = opposite
adj = adjacent
hyp = hypotenuse

15. Relating the Trigonometric Functions

When you know the value of just one of the trigonometric functions, you can find all the others using the Pythagorean theorem.

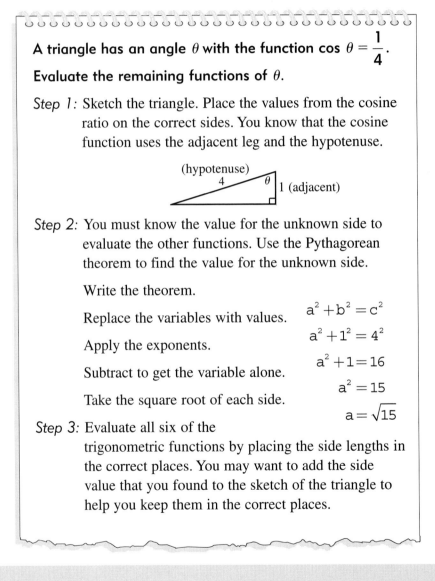

A triangle has an angle θ with the function $\cos \theta = \dfrac{1}{4}$.

Evaluate the remaining functions of θ.

Step 1: Sketch the triangle. Place the values from the cosine ratio on the correct sides. You know that the cosine function uses the adjacent leg and the hypotenuse.

(hypotenuse)
4 θ 1 (adjacent)

Step 2: You must know the value for the unknown side to evaluate the other functions. Use the Pythagorean theorem to find the value for the unknown side.

Write the theorem.
Replace the variables with values.
Apply the exponents.
Subtract to get the variable alone.
Take the square root of each side.

$$a^2 + b^2 = c^2$$
$$a^2 + 1^2 = 4^2$$
$$a^2 + 1 = 16$$
$$a^2 = 15$$
$$a = \sqrt{15}$$

Step 3: Evaluate all six of the trigonometric functions by placing the side lengths in the correct places. You may want to add the side value that you found to the sketch of the triangle to help you keep them in the correct places.

Remember: Radicals are numbers that are under the radical sign. Chapter 9 has more about square roots and radicals.

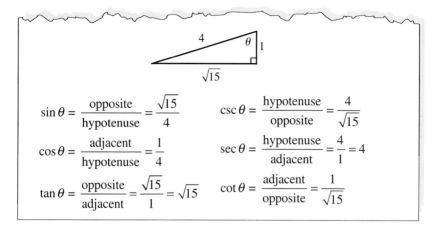

$$\sin \theta = \frac{\text{opposite}}{\text{hypotenuse}} = \frac{\sqrt{15}}{4}$$

$$\csc \theta = \frac{\text{hypotenuse}}{\text{opposite}} = \frac{4}{\sqrt{15}}$$

$$\cos \theta = \frac{\text{adjacent}}{\text{hypotenuse}} = \frac{1}{4}$$

$$\sec \theta = \frac{\text{hypotenuse}}{\text{adjacent}} = \frac{4}{1} = 4$$

$$\tan \theta = \frac{\text{opposite}}{\text{adjacent}} = \frac{\sqrt{15}}{1} = \sqrt{15}$$

$$\cot \theta = \frac{\text{adjacent}}{\text{opposite}} = \frac{1}{\sqrt{15}}$$

Sometimes a ratio may be given as a whole number. For example, in the problem above, sec $\theta = 4$. All of the functions are ratios, by their definitions. To say that tan $\theta = 2$ is saying that the opposite side in relation to the adjacent side is in a ratio of 2 to 1, because $2 = \frac{2}{1}$.

In a right triangle, csc θ = 3. Find the sine of θ.

Step 1: Decide what side values you know and what values you need to know.

The cosecant function uses the ratio of the hypotenuse to the opposite in the ratio of 3 to 1. The value for the hypotenuse is 3, and the value for the opposite leg is 1.

The sine function uses the opposite leg and the hypotenuse. These are values that you already know from the cosecant function.

Step 2: Evaluate the sine function.

$$\sin \theta = \frac{\text{opposite}}{\text{hypotenuse}} = \frac{1}{3}$$

Wow, Pythagoras was one cool dude!

16. Complements and Cofunctions

As you learned on page 20, the two acute angles in any right triangle add up to 90 degrees. Two angles that add up to 90 degrees are called complements (page 9.) For any right triangle then, if one of the acute angles is θ, the other acute angle must be $90° - \theta$.

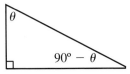

For each of the following angles, find the complementary angle.

a. **32°**   b. **67°**   c. **19°**   d. **45°**

Step 1: Write a general equation that will work for each of the angle values. Complementary angles must total 90°, so if you subtract the known angle from 90°, you will be left with the measure of the second angle.

$$90 - \theta = \text{the unknown angle.}$$

Step 2: Substitute each angle value for θ to find each complementary angle.

a. $90° - 32° = 58°$

b. $90° - 67° = 23°$

c. $90° - 19° = 71°$

d. $90° - 45° = 45°$

Complementary angles have a sum of 90°.
Supplementary angles have a sum of 180°.

Cofunctions

There are three pairs of trigonometric cofunctions.

Sine	and	*Cosine*
Secant	and	*Cosecant*
Tangent	and	*Cotangent*

Look at the relationship between sine and cosine in the triangle below.

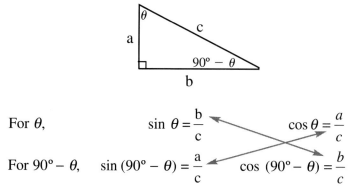

For θ, $\qquad\qquad\qquad \sin\theta = \dfrac{b}{c} \qquad\qquad\qquad \cos\theta = \dfrac{a}{c}$

For $90° - \theta$, $\quad \sin(90° - \theta) = \dfrac{a}{c} \qquad \cos(90° - \theta) = \dfrac{b}{c}$

The sine of an angle θ has the same value as the cosine of an angle $90 - \theta$. The cosine of an angle θ has the same value as the sine of an angle $90 - \theta$. Trigonometric functions of an angle have the same value as the cofunctions of its complement.

Name the equal complementary cofunction of csc 32°.

Step 1: Write an equation that sets the first trigonometric ratio equal to the cofunction of its complement.

$$\csc 32° = \sec(90° - 32°) = \sec 58°$$

In a right triangle, the opposite side to one acute angle is the adjacent side to the other acute angle.

17. Reciprocal Identities

Fractions that are "flipped" are called reciprocals. When reciprocals are multiplied, the product is 1.

Sine and cosecant are reciprocal functions. When a sine ratio is multiplied by the cosecant ratio, the result is 1.

$$\frac{\text{opp}}{\text{hyp}} \times \frac{\text{hyp}}{\text{opp}} = 1$$

$$\sin\theta \times \csc\theta = 1$$

$$\csc\theta = \frac{1}{\sin\theta}$$

This equation, $\csc\theta = \dfrac{1}{\sin\theta}$, is called a reciprocal identity.

You can use reciprocal identities to find the value of reciprocal functions.

---

sin 30° = 0.5 **Find csc 30°.**

Step 1: Write the reciprocal identity that uses sine and cosecant.

$$\csc\theta = \frac{1}{\sin\theta}$$

Step 2: Replace the variables with the values that you know. The angle measure is 30°.

$$\csc 30° = \frac{1}{0.5}$$

Step 3: Solve for csc 30°.

$$\csc 30° = \frac{1}{0.5}$$

$$\csc 30° = 2$$

---

reciprocals—Two fractions that, when multiplied, have a product of 1. The fractions $\dfrac{2}{3}$ and $\dfrac{3}{2}$ are reciprocals. $\dfrac{2}{3} \times \dfrac{3}{2} = 1.$

Write the reciprocal identity for secant. Show how you arrived at the identity.

Step 1: Decide what other trigonometric ratio uses the same sides as the secant function.

Secant uses the hypotenuse and the adjacent leg. The other trigonometric ratio that uses these sides is cosine.

Step 2: Reciprocal identities must have a product of 1. Cosine and secant are reciprocal functions Write the two ratios in an equation that equals 1. First write the equation showing the ratios, then change to the ratio names.

$$\frac{adj}{hyp} \times \frac{hyp}{adj} = 1$$

$$\cos\theta \times \sec\theta = 1$$

Step 3: Divide both sides of the equation by cos to get sec by itself.

$$\frac{\cancel{\cos\theta} \times \sec\theta}{\cancel{\cos\theta}} = \frac{1}{\cos\theta}$$

$$\sec\theta = \frac{1}{\cos\theta}$$

The reciprocal identity is $\sec\theta = \dfrac{1}{\cos\theta}$.

Cotangent and tangent are also reciprocal functions.

$$\cot\theta = \frac{1}{\tan\theta}$$

$$\sin\theta = \frac{1}{\csc\theta} \qquad \csc\theta = \frac{1}{\sin\theta} \qquad \cos\theta = \frac{1}{\sec\theta}$$

$$\sec\theta = \frac{1}{\cos\theta} \qquad \tan\theta = \frac{1}{\cot\theta} \qquad \cot\theta = \frac{1}{\tan\theta}$$

18. Trigonometry Tables and Calculators

All of the trigonometric ratios are constant for a given angle. No matter what the side length, the sine ratio for an angle of 30° is always 0.5. This is true for all trigonometric ratios and for all angles. You can find the value for the trigonometric ratios in two ways.

Trigonometry Tables

Trigonometry tables can be found in mathematics textbooks that use trigonometry, as well as in many engineering, machinery, and mechanics books. The trigonometry table can also be found easily on the Internet. The table below is only a small part of the entire table.

To find the value for a trigonometric ratio, first locate the angle in either the left- or right-hand column. Then move across the row to the correct ratio.

The value for tan 12° is 0.212557.

Angle	Sine	Cosine	Tangent	Secant	Cosecant	Cotangent	Angle
10	0.173648	0.984808	0.176327	1.015427	5.758770	5.671282	10
11	0.190809	0.981627	0.194380	1.018717	5.240843	5.14554	11
12	0.207912	0.978148	0.212557	1.022341	4.809734	4.704630	12
13	0.224951	0.974370	0.230868	1.026304	4.445411	4.331476	13
14	0.241922	0.970296	0.249328	1.030614	4.133565	4.010781	14
15	0.258819	0.965926	0.267949	1.035276	3.863703	3.732051	15
16	0.275637	0.961262	0.286745	1.040299	3.627955	3.487414	16
17	0.292372	0.956305	0.305731	1.045692	3.420304	3.270853	17
18	0.309017	0.951057	0.324920	1.051462	3.236068	3.077684	18
19	0.325568	0.945519	0.344328	1.057621	3.071553	2.904211	19

Trigonometry tables can be used to find an angle from a ratio, or a ratio from an angle.

You can also use a trigonometry table to find the angle when you know the ratio.

Find the value in degrees of θ when sec θ= 1.052.

Step 1: Find the secant column on a trigonometry table.

Step 2: Follow the column up or down until you find the value closest to 1.052.

Using the table on page 40, sec 18° = 1.051462, and sec 19° = 1.057621. The closer value is 1.051462.

$\theta \approx 18°$

Calculators

Trigonometric ratios can also be found using a calculator. Most calculators have trigonometric function buttons for sine, cosine, and tangent. Others include secant, cosecant, and cotangent. Enter the angle's measure, then press the button for the ratio you want to find.

You can find an angle's measure by using a calculator. You need a calculator with buttons that are labeled with the ratio followed by $^{-1}$, for example, $\sin^{-1}$. These are called inverse buttons and will find the angle measure from a ratio value.

Use a calculator to find the value in degrees of θ when tan θ = 2.

Step 1: Type in the number 2, followed by the $\tan^{-1}$ button. Round the value to the nearest tenth.

$\theta = \tan^{-1} 2 \approx 63.4$

On calculators that do not have secant, cosecant, and cotangent functions, you can use the reciprocal identities from Chapter 17 to find the value of the ratios.

19. Sine, Cosecant, and Side Length

For a right triangle, when you know an acute angle and one of the side lengths, you can find any of the other measurements.

The sine and cosecant functions use three measures:
- the angle measure
- the length of the opposite leg
- the length of the hypotenuse

$$\sin\theta = \frac{\text{opp}}{\text{hyp}} \qquad \csc\theta = \frac{\text{hyp}}{\text{opp}}$$

You can use the sine or cosecant function to find one of the measurements if you know the other two.

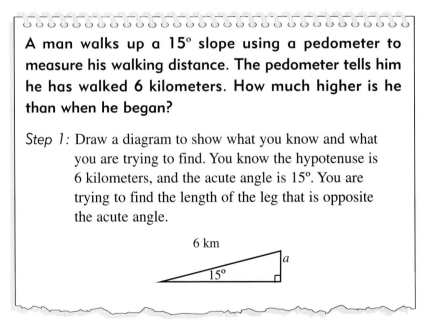

A man walks up a 15° slope using a pedometer to measure his walking distance. The pedometer tells him he has walked 6 kilometers. How much higher is he than when he began?

Step 1: Draw a diagram to show what you know and what you are trying to find. You know the hypotenuse is 6 kilometers, and the acute angle is 15°. You are trying to find the length of the leg that is opposite the acute angle.

6 km

15°

a

Sine and cosecant are called reciprocal functions because their ratios are the reciprocals of each other.

Step 2: Decide which of the trigonometric functions you can use. You know the angle and hypotenuse. You are trying to find the opposite leg. The functions sine and cosecant use the angle, opposite, and hypotenuse.

$$\sin\theta = \frac{\text{opp}}{\text{hyp}} \qquad \csc\theta = \frac{\text{hyp}}{\text{opp}}$$

When the opposite leg is the unknown value, the sine function is easier to solve, because the opposite leg can be found by multiplying both sides by the hypotenuse.

Step 3: Place the known values into the trigonometric function for sine.

$$\sin 15° = \frac{a}{6}$$

Step 4: Find the sine of 15° using the trigonometric table or a calculator. Substitute in the value. The value is rounded, so use the approximately equal to sign, $\approx$.

Step 5: Solve for *a.*

$$0.2588 \approx \frac{a}{6}$$

Multiply both sides by 6 to get *a* alone.

$$1.5528 \approx a$$

The man is about 1.55 kilometers higher than he was when he began walking.

Use the cosecant function when you are trying to find the length of the hypotenuse.

Many solutions in trigonometric problems will have rounded answers. Use the $\approx$ sign when you round your answer.

20. Cosine, Secant, and Side Length

The cosine and secant functions are reciprocal functions that show the relationship between the acute angle measure and the lengths of the adjacent leg and the hypotenuse.

$$\cos\theta = \frac{adj}{hyp}$$

$$\sec\theta = \frac{hyp}{adj}$$

You can use the cosine or secant function to find one of the measurements if you know the other two.

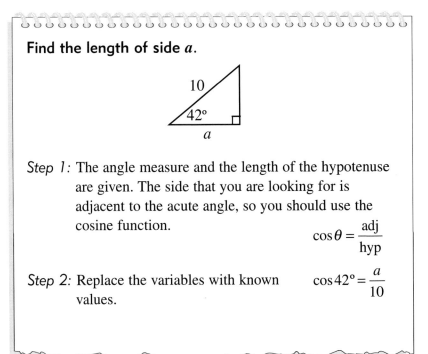

Find the length of side a.

Step 1: The angle measure and the length of the hypotenuse are given. The side that you are looking for is adjacent to the acute angle, so you should use the cosine function.

$$\cos\theta = \frac{adj}{hyp}$$

Step 2: Replace the variables with known values.

$$\cos 42° = \frac{a}{10}$$

The cosine and secant functions both use the adjacent leg and the hypotenuse in their ratios.

Step 3: Find the value for cos 42° using the trigonometry table or a calculator.

$$0.7431 \approx \frac{a}{10}$$

Step 4: Solve for *a*.

$$7.43 \approx a$$

Problems that have the angle measure and the adjacent leg length use the secant function to find the hypotenuse length.

To reach a certain window, a ladder is placed at a 50° angle, 8 feet away from the base of the house. How long is the ladder?

Step 1: Draw a diagram to help you decide what you know and what you are trying to find.

You know the angle and the adjacent leg. You are trying to find the hypotenuse.

Step 2: Use the secant function.

$$\sec \theta = \frac{\text{hyp}}{\text{adj}}$$

Replace the variables with the known values.

$$\sec 50° = \frac{c}{8}$$

Step 3: Find the secant of 50 using the trigonometry table or a calculator.

$$1.5557 \approx \frac{c}{8}$$

Step 4: Solve for *c*.

$$12.45 \approx c$$

The ladder is about 12.45 feet long.

You may find it easier to solve for a missing numerator than a missing denominator. Keep this in mind when you are deciding which trigonometric ratio to use to find a missing side length.

21. Tangent, Cotangent, and Side Length

The tangent and cotangent functions are the most used trigonometric functions in the real world. They are applied in science, architecture, and engineering every day.

The tangent and cotangent functions relate the opposite and adjacent legs of a right triangle, and one acute angle. When one leg and an acute angle are known, you can find the measurement of the unknown leg.

$$\tan \theta = \frac{\text{opp}}{\text{adj}}$$

$$\cot \theta = \frac{\text{adj}}{\text{opp}}$$

A model rocket travels straight up from a launchpad. At one time, an observer from a point **200 feet** from the launchpad sees the rocket's nose from a **60°** angle. What is the distance at that time from the nose of the rocket to the launchpad?

Step 1: Draw a diagram to help you decide what you know and what you are trying to find.

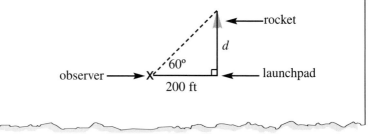

Tangent and cotangent are both cofunctions and reciprocal functions.

You know the angle is a 60° angle. You also know the adjacent leg to the acute angle is 200 feet.

You are trying to find the length of the opposite leg.

Step 2: Use the tangent function.

$$\tan \theta = \frac{\text{opp}}{\text{adj}}$$

Replace the variables with known values.

$$\tan 60° = \frac{d}{200}$$

Step 3: Find the value for tan 60° using the trigonometry table or a calculator.

$$1.732 \approx \frac{d}{200}$$

Step 4: Solve for *d*.

$$346.4 \approx d$$

The rocket's nose is approximately 346.4 feet from the launchpad.

The cotangent function can be used when you know the opposite leg and the acute angle and you are trying to find the adjacent leg in a right triangle.

The tangent and cotangent functions are cofunctions. In the example, the value for the tangent of a 60-degree angle is about 1.732. The complementary angle to a 60-degree angle is 30 degrees, so the cotangent of a 30-degree angle is also about 1.732.

$$\tan 60° = \cot 30°$$
$$1.732 = 1.732$$

Complements and cofunctions are covered in Chapter 16.

22. Finding the Angle Measure

When you know the length of any two sides of a right triangle, you can find the angle measure for either acute angle.

A road leads directly up the side of a hill. The bottom of the hill is at sea level, and the top of the hill is at 5,000 feet. The road up the hill is 21,000 feet long from the bottom of the hill to the top. What is the inclination of the road?

Step 1: Draw a diagram to show what you know and what you are trying to find.

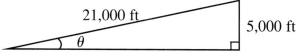

21,000 ft 5,000 ft θ

You know the hypotenuse of the triangle that is formed, and you know the length of the side that is opposite the angle you are trying to find.

Step 2: Decide what trigonometric ratio you can use to find the angle. Sine and cosecant use opposite and hypotenuse. Use the function for sine. Replace the variables with known values.

$$\sin \theta = \frac{\text{opp}}{\text{hyp}}$$

$$\sin \theta = \frac{5,000}{21,000}$$

Step 3: Divide.

$$\sin \theta \approx 0.238095$$

Step 4: Use a calculator or a trigonometry table to find the closest value for sine.

$$\theta \approx \sin^{-1} 0.238095$$

$$\theta \approx 13.8°$$

The inclination is about 13.8°.

Using the trigonometry table or your calculator to find the angle is covered in Chapter 18.

Elevation and Depression

Heights are sometimes measured using the angle of elevation or the angle of depression.

If you are looking up to see an object, the angle from a horizontal line to your line of sight is called the angle of elevation.

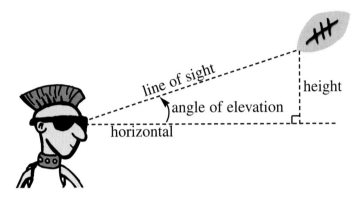

When you are looking down to see an object, the angle made with the horizontal is called the angle of depression.

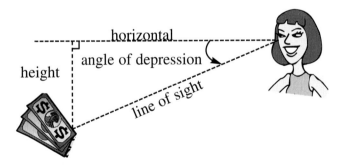

Angles of elevation are angled up from a straight line.
Angles of depression are angled down from a straight line.
The length of the leg opposite these angles in a right triangle will be the height.

23. The Trigonometric Identities

The Pythagorean theorem states that for every right triangle, $a^2 + b^2 = c^2$ when a and b are the leg lengths and c is the length of the hypotenuse. In relation to the acute angle, the legs a and b are called the opposite and adjacent legs.

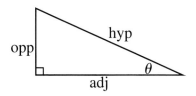

Using the terms *opposite*, *adjacent*, and *hypotenuse* in place of the variables, the Pythagorean theorem can be written:

$$opp^2 + adj^2 = hyp^2$$

To get a 1 on the right side of the equation, you can divide both sides of the equation by hyp^2. Treat opp, adj, and hyp as any other variables.

$$\frac{opp^2}{hyp^2} + \frac{adj^2}{hyp^2} = \frac{\cancel{hyp^2}}{\cancel{hyp^2}} = 1$$

Notice the first ratio in the equation is the square of the sine ratio. This can be written as $\sin^2\theta$. The second ratio is equal to $\cos^2\theta$. Replace the ratios with their ratio names to get a trigonometric identity.

$$\sin^2\theta + \cos^2\theta = 1$$

The reciprocal and cofunction properties and the identities on these pages are very important for figuring out trigonometric problems.

Two other identities that use the Pythagorean theorem are important in trigonometry.

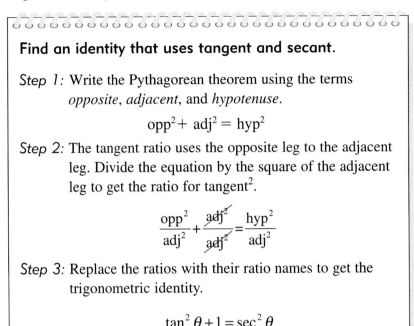

Find an identity that uses tangent and secant.

Step 1: Write the Pythagorean theorem using the terms *opposite*, *adjacent*, and *hypotenuse*.

$$\text{opp}^2 + \text{adj}^2 = \text{hyp}^2$$

Step 2: The tangent ratio uses the opposite leg to the adjacent leg. Divide the equation by the square of the adjacent leg to get the ratio for tangent^2.

$$\frac{\text{opp}^2}{\text{adj}^2} + \frac{\cancel{\text{adj}^2}}{\cancel{\text{adj}^2}} = \frac{\text{hyp}^2}{\text{adj}^2}$$

Step 3: Replace the ratios with their ratio names to get the trigonometric identity.

$$\tan^2\theta + 1 = \sec^2\theta$$

The third identity that is found by using the Pythagorean theorem is

$$1 + \cot^2\theta = \csc^2\theta$$

Identities make it easier to solve problems.

Not only are the sides of a right triangle related according to trigonometric functions, but the functions themselves are also related.

24. Isosceles Right Triangles

A right triangle that has two 45° angles is called an isosceles right triangle. *Isosceles* means "equal legs." The two legs are the same length, which makes the two acute angles the same measure. Since the sum of two acute angles must be 90°, and 90° ÷ 2 = 45°, you know the angles for an isosceles right triangle are 45°, 45°, and 90°.

The hypotenuse in a right triangle is always longer than the legs, so the two legs are the sides that are equal in length.

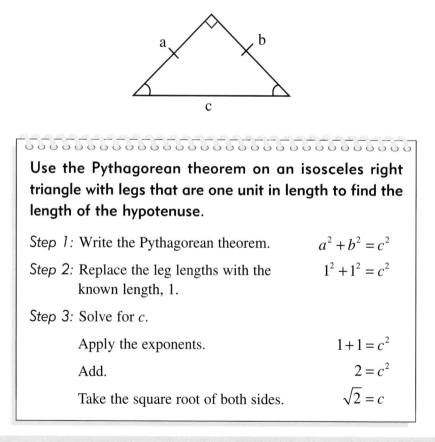

Use the Pythagorean theorem on an isosceles right triangle with legs that are one unit in length to find the length of the hypotenuse.

Step 1: Write the Pythagorean theorem. $\qquad a^2 + b^2 = c^2$

Step 2: Replace the leg lengths with the $\qquad 1^2 + 1^2 = c^2$
known length, 1.

Step 3: Solve for c.

Apply the exponents. $\qquad 1 + 1 = c^2$

Add. $\qquad 2 = c^2$

Take the square root of both sides. $\qquad \sqrt{2} = c$

The sides of the 45-45-90 triangle are in the ratio $1:1:\sqrt{2}$. This special ratio is one that should be memorized.

Solving the Isosceles Right Triangle

Solving a triangle means you know all three sides and all three angles. In the isosceles right triangle, you already know all of the angles. By using the proportion you just found, you can easily find all of the sides.

All triangles that have congruent angles are similar. Similar triangles have corresponding sides that are in proportion. All isosceles right triangles will have sides that are in the proportion $1:1:\sqrt{2}$.

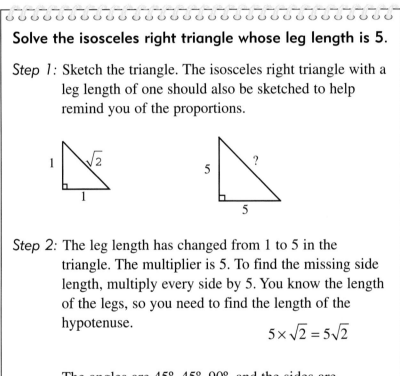

Solve the isosceles right triangle whose leg length is 5.

Step 1: Sketch the triangle. The isosceles right triangle with a leg length of one should also be sketched to help remind you of the proportions.

Step 2: The leg length has changed from 1 to 5 in the triangle. The multiplier is 5. To find the missing side length, multiply every side by 5. You know the length of the legs, so you need to find the length of the hypotenuse.

$$5 \times \sqrt{2} = 5\sqrt{2}$$

The angles are 45°, 45°, 90°, and the sides are $5 : 5 : 5\sqrt{2}$

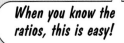

When you know the ratios, this is easy!

25. 30-60-90 Triangles

Triangles whose angles are 30°, 60°, and 90° have many special properties. Like an isosceles right triangle, the sides of a 30-60-90 triangle are in proportions that make it easy to work with.

The 30-60-90 is half of an equilateral triangle. In an equilateral triangle, all of the sides are equal length and all of the angles are equal measure. All of the angles are 60° angles (180° ÷ 3 = 60°).

If you draw an equilateral triangle that has a side length of 2 units, you can divide it in half to find the proportions for all 30-60-90 triangles. The hypotenuse is 2 units, and the shorter leg is half of the hypotenuse, 1 unit. The Pythagorean theorem gives a length of $\sqrt{3}$ for the longer leg.

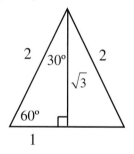

If the short leg on a 30-60-90 triangle is 2, you know that you have changed the proportions by multiplying by 2, so the hypotenuse is 2 × 2 = 4, and the longer leg is $2 \times \sqrt{3} = 2\sqrt{3}$.

isosceles right triangle—A right triangle with legs that are the same length.

equilateral triangle—A triangle with all three sides the same length.

Special Triangles and Trigonometry

For any problem that uses an isosceles right triangle or the 30-60-90 triangle, you should never have to use a calculator or the trigonometry table to find the trigonometric ratios.

Evaluate the six trigonometric ratios for a 45° and a 60° angle.

Step 1: Sketch the special triangles and show their side ratios.

Step 2: Use the special triangles and their side lengths to find the trigonometric ratios for a 45° and a 60° angle.

$$\sin 45° = \frac{\text{opp}}{\text{hyp}} = \frac{1}{\sqrt{2}} = \frac{\sqrt{2}}{2} \qquad \sin 60° = \frac{\text{opp}}{\text{hyp}} = \frac{\sqrt{3}}{2}$$

$$\cos 45° = \frac{\text{adj}}{\text{hyp}} = \frac{1}{\sqrt{2}} = \frac{\sqrt{2}}{2} \qquad \cos 60° = \frac{\text{adj}}{\text{hyp}} = \frac{1}{2}$$

$$\tan 45° = \frac{\text{opp}}{\text{adj}} = \frac{1}{1} = 1 \qquad \tan 60° = \frac{\text{opp}}{\text{adj}} = \frac{\sqrt{3}}{1} = \sqrt{3}$$

$$\csc 45° = \frac{\text{hyp}}{\text{opp}} = \frac{\sqrt{2}}{1} = \sqrt{2} \qquad \csc 60° = \frac{\text{hyp}}{\text{opp}} = \frac{2}{\sqrt{3}} = \frac{2\sqrt{3}}{3}$$

$$\sec 45° = \frac{\text{hyp}}{\text{adj}} = \frac{\sqrt{2}}{1} = \sqrt{2} \qquad \sec 60° = \frac{\text{hyp}}{\text{adj}} = \frac{2}{1} = 2$$

$$\cot 45° = \frac{\text{adj}}{\text{opp}} = \frac{1}{1} = 1 \qquad \cot 60° = \frac{\text{adj}}{\text{opp}} = \frac{1}{\sqrt{3}} = \frac{\sqrt{3}}{3}$$

Ratios should never be left with radicals in the denominator. Move them to the numerator by multiplying the numerator and denominator by the same radical.

$$\frac{1}{\sqrt{2}} \times \frac{\sqrt{2}}{\sqrt{2}} = \frac{\sqrt{2}}{2}$$

26. The Unit Circle

Trigonometry sometimes uses a circle with a radius of one unit to describe the measurement of angles. This circle is called the unit circle. The center of the unit circle is on the origin, which is the point (0, 0).

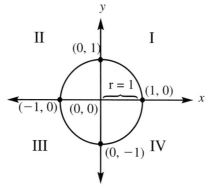

The unit circle is divided into four areas called quadrants. The quadrants are named in a counterclockwise direction using Roman numerals. Quadrant I is in the top right corner, where both the x-values and y-values are positive. In the next chapter, you will see how the x and y values affect the trigonometric functions.

The Unit Circle in Trigonometry

So far, you have seen how the trigonometric functions work for a right triangle. Trigonometry can also be used with angles that are not part of a right triangle by relating the angle to a right triangle on the unit circle. The acute angle formed at the origin is called the related angle.

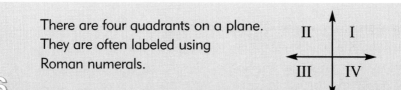

There are four quadrants on a plane. They are often labeled using Roman numerals.

Begin with the vertex of the angle on the origin of the unit circle and the initial side of the angle on the positive x-axis. When the terminal side of the angle is in the first quadrant, the angle has a measurement between 0° and 90°. Draw a line from the x-axis to the point where the second ray crosses the unit circle.

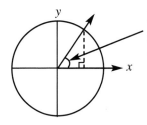

In the first quadrant, the related angle is the same as the original angle.

The same thing is done with angles that are larger than 90 degrees. Draw an imaginary line from the point where the terminal side crosses the unit circle to the x-axis. Angles between 90° and 180° are in the second quadrant.

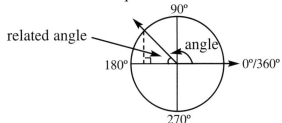

Angles between 180° and 270° are in the third quadrant, and angles between 270° and 360° are in the fourth quadrant.

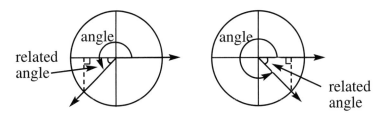

You can draw a related right triangle on the unit circle for any angle, so that you can use the trigonometric functions to find unknown measurements.

---

initial side of an angle—The side of an angle where you begin measuring the angle's size.
terminal side of an angle—The side of an angle where you stop measuring the angle's size.

27. Signs of Trigonometric Functions

When trigonometric functions are used for angles that are not part of a right triangle, the quadrant where the related triangle falls tells you if the trigonometric ratio is positive or negative.

$$(-,+) \quad | \quad (+,+)$$

$$(-,-) \quad | \quad (+,-)$$

Angles between 0° and 90° are in the first quadrant. All of the side lengths of the related triangle are positive. All of the trigonometric functions are also positive. Look at the 45° angle below.

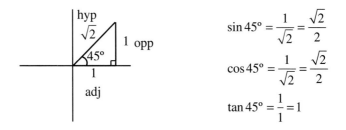

$$\sin 45° = \frac{1}{\sqrt{2}} = \frac{\sqrt{2}}{2}$$

$$\cos 45° = \frac{1}{\sqrt{2}} = \frac{\sqrt{2}}{2}$$

$$\tan 45° = \frac{1}{1} = 1$$

Angles that are between 90° and 180° are in the second quadrant. In the second quadrant, the related angle is 180° − θ. The adjacent leg is a negative value. The hypotenuse is always a positive value. Look at the 135° angle at the top of the next page.

The trigonometric functions remain the same for each quadrant; the only difference is whether they are positive or negative.

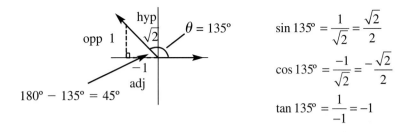

$$\sin 135° = \frac{1}{\sqrt{2}} = \frac{\sqrt{2}}{2}$$

$$\cos 135° = \frac{-1}{\sqrt{2}} = \frac{-\sqrt{2}}{2}$$

$$\tan 135° = \frac{1}{-1} = -1$$

In the third quadrant, the related angle is $\theta - 180°$. The adjacent and opposite sides of the related right triangle are both negative. The ratios for sine and cosine are negative. Both of the values used for the tangent function are negative, which results in a positive ratio. Look at the 225° angle below.

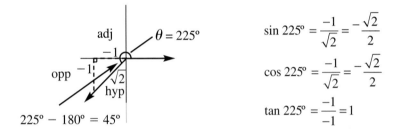

$$\sin 225° = \frac{-1}{\sqrt{2}} = -\frac{\sqrt{2}}{2}$$

$$\cos 225° = \frac{-1}{\sqrt{2}} = -\frac{\sqrt{2}}{2}$$

$$\tan 225° = \frac{-1}{-1} = 1$$

In the fourth quadrant, the related angle is $360° - \theta$. The adjacent side of the related right triangle is positive, and the opposite side is negative. The sine and tangent functions are negative, but the cosine function is positive. Look at the 315° angle below.

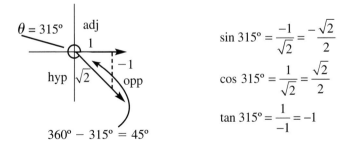

$$\sin 315° = \frac{-1}{\sqrt{2}} = -\frac{\sqrt{2}}{2}$$

$$\cos 315° = \frac{1}{\sqrt{2}} = \frac{\sqrt{2}}{2}$$

$$\tan 315° = \frac{1}{-1} = -1$$

The hypotenuse is always a positive value when you are finding the sign of a trigonometric function.

28. Radians and Degrees

Radians

Every circle has a radius, *r*, which is the distance from the center of the circle to any point on the circle. The circumference of a circle is the distance around the circle, starting at a point and following the circle back to the same point. In geometry, you learn that the circumference of a circle has a length of $2\pi r$.

The circumference of the unit circle is found by substituting in the radius length of 1 for the variable *r*. So, the circumference of a unit circle is $2\pi(1) = 2\pi$. The radian measure is the length of the section of the unit circle that is inside the angle.

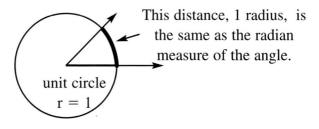

This distance, 1 radius, is the same as the radian measure of the angle.

unit circle
r = 1

Degrees to Radians

In degree measure, one revolution around a circle is 360°.
$$360° = 2\pi \text{ radians}$$

Half a revolution around the circle is 180°.
Half of 2π is π. So,
$$180° = \pi \text{ radians}$$

The number of degrees in an angle can be converted into radians by multiplying it by $\dfrac{\pi}{180}$ radians.

$$\frac{\pi}{180} \text{ radian} = 1° \qquad 1 \text{ radian} = \frac{180°}{\pi}$$

When the measurement of an angle is given in radians, the word *radian* is often left off. Whenever you see an angle measurement that uses the symbol π, you know the measurement is in radians.

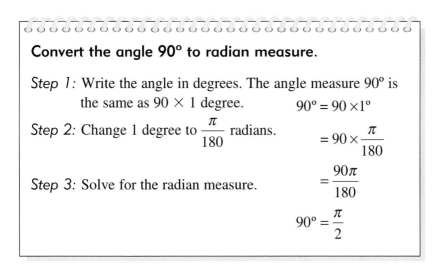

Convert the angle 90° to radian measure.

Step 1: Write the angle in degrees. The angle measure 90° is the same as 90 × 1 degree.

$$90° = 90 \times 1°$$

Step 2: Change 1 degree to $\dfrac{\pi}{180}$ radians.

$$= 90 \times \dfrac{\pi}{180}$$

Step 3: Solve for the radian measure.

$$= \dfrac{90\pi}{180}$$

$$90° = \dfrac{\pi}{2}$$

Radians to Degrees

When radians need to be changed to degrees, use the fact that one radian is equal to $\dfrac{180°}{\pi}$.

Convert $\dfrac{3\pi}{2}$ radians to degrees.

Step 1: Write the angle in radians.

$$\dfrac{3\pi}{2} = \dfrac{3\pi}{2} \times 1 \text{ radian}$$

Step 2: Change 1 radian to $\dfrac{180}{\pi}$ degrees.

$$= \dfrac{3\pi}{2} \times \dfrac{180°}{\pi}$$

Step 3: Solve for the degree measure.

The πs will cancel. Reduce, then multiply.

$$= \dfrac{3\cancel{\pi}}{\cancel{2}} \times \dfrac{\cancel{180°}^{90°}}{\cancel{\pi}}$$

$$= 270°$$

Radian measurement can be shown on a ruler and used for distance. Degrees do not measure distance.
Radians make many calculations simpler than using degrees, minutes, and seconds.

Further Reading

Books

Ayres, Frank, Jr., and Robert E. Moyer. *Shaum's Easy Outline of Trigonometry*. New York: McGraw-Hill Trade, 2002.

Caron, Lucille, and Philip M. St. Jacques. *Geometry*. Berkeley Heights, N.J.: Enslow Publishers, Inc., 2001.

Gibillisco, Stan. *Trigonometry Demystified*. New York: McGraw-Hill/TAB Electronics, 2003.

Internet Addresses

The Math Forum. *Ask Dr. Math*. © 1994–2003. <http://mathforum.org/dr.math>

MathMedics. *S.O.S. Mathematics Trigonometry*. © 1999–2003. <http://www.sosmath.com/trig/trig.html>

Spector, Lawrence. *Topics in Trigonometry*. © 2000–2003. <http://www.themathpage.com>

Trigonometry. *MathTV*. © 2000. <http:www.mathtv.com>

Index